Eco-minimalism
the antidote to eco-bling

Howard Liddell

RIBA ⊞ **Publishing**

© Howard Liddell, 2008

Published by RIBA Publishing Ltd
15 Bonhill Street, London EC2P 2EA

ISBN 978 1 85946 300 0

Stock Code 65488

British Library Cataloguing in Publications Data

A catalogue record for this book is available
from the British Library.

Author: **Howard Liddell**

Publisher: **Steven Cross**

Commissioning Editor: **Matthew Thompson**

Project Editor: **Susan George**

Copy-editor: **Ian McDonald**

Designed by **Kneath Associates**

Typeset, printed and bound by
Latimer Trend Co Ltd, Plymouth

RIBA Publishing is part of RIBA Enterprises Ltd.

www.ribaenterprises.com

Cover photo: **Howard Liddell**

contents

Foreword

By Robin Harper

Buildings and construction between them contribute between 25% and 45 % of all global warming gases, and a fair amount of other secondary pollution. At the beginning of this century we can now see that if we do not want to increase the temperature of the planet beyond the serious danger point of a 2 degree rise in average global temperatures, we need to cut our greenhouse gases by 80% by 2050, and every single sector must make the maximum contribution possible.

This comprehensive study of the way forward cuts through the usual objections of cost, lack of technology, restricted choice of materials, and all the other excuses put forward by the construction industry, and shows how simple easy to do improvements in insulation, air tightness, building materials and techniques that any one can learn will give us high quality low tech super energy efficient houses that will stay efficient throughout their lifetimes with a minimum of maintenance and repair.
Too good to be true? Read on.

From the first sentence of the introduction to the basic sums at the end, this book takes the planner, builder, architect, designer, building controller, and politician and leads them painlessly to the conclusion that we can with a little imagination and will, find a way to provide buildings that are value for money and fit for purpose in a world of rising temperatures and rising fuel costs, that are likely to stay high for all time.

Between the turn of the century and today it has become more apparent with every scientific paper published, every book written, every speech given, that climate change is upon us, and simply trying to manage energy generation sustainable can only solve a fraction of the problem. Energy demand reduction is the quickest, surest, and most secure way of achieving our goal of a stable climate future. We absolutely have to embody maximum embedded energy conservation in everything we build, make, use, and re use.

We also need low carbon cost materials and building methods, and must always look for value for money in every thing we think of doing, and not allow ourselves to be distracted by inefficient or poorly placed technologies. The mass building sector really ought to take this book to heart, because it shows how they could get started on making their contribution right now, without waiting for new rules or regulations or grants. In the present situation it should be only too easy to sell houses that cost only a fraction more than the market, if even that, but which save thousands of pounds in heating bills over their lifetimes, and are healthy and comfortable to live in. This book shows us how to do it! Read every word!

Glencoe Visitor Centre.

Gaia Architects. Photo Michael Wolshover

Preface

The idea for this book dates from the turn of the century (20th/21st), and the first article on the topic, for which I dreamt up the seemingly unlikely title of 'Eco-minimalism', was published in 2002 in the SEDA[1] quarterly magazine. I then linked up with Nick Grant, a like-minded co-member of AECB,[2] for a joint article in their journal the following year.

The article was intended for the 'green insider' architects and builders (SEDA & AECB members) as a warning that if we didn't confront some harsh 'triple bottom line' realities and crunch some numbers, then our missionary zeal would be undermined by the sceptics who would.

Firstly, I found the approach was anything but a mere insider's critique. It had mileage out on the platforms of every conference centre and community-hall gathering I attended for the ensuing year and, evidently, its message was bridging the gap between the 'green-realists' and the 'every person' on the Clapham omnibus.

Secondly, I forgot where I came into this whole game 30 years ago – through 'alternative technology' – and that when green eventually became cool (a couple of years ago in the UK), the novice converts followed the same path and were less likely – not more – to crunch numbers than the OAP greenies. Our cries of 'Well we did this back in the 70s and ...' went unheeded as a new, self-confident but blinkered generation insisted on reinventing the green technological wheel.

So the need for this piece of work is, I feel, just as pressing as I originally thought – and perhaps even more so, but for a different set of reasons.

It's all rather a positive outcome – a book not for the few, but for everyone.

Howard Liddell
Gaia Architects, Edinburgh
July 2008

1 Scottish Ecological Design Association.

2 Association of Environmentally Conscious Builders.

Ludesch Centre.

Photo Howard Liddell

Acknowledgements

In terms of the Bruntland definition of sustainability – providing for the needs of the present generation without compromising those of future generations – I hope my children will forgive being deprived of their rightful amount of quality father-time whilst I have tilted at windmills, vainly seeking planetary improvement. If so, thanks to them, and to their much-loved Granny Alys – my late mother – who wasted nothing, recycled everything, adored simplicity and was damn good company. Thanks, also, to Auntie May for saying 'a day without learning is a day wasted'.

As for those from whom I have been learning daily – since this is my first major book, I get the opportunity to thank 30-years' worth of 'fellow green travellers' for their influence, company and (always the most welcome) humour. Indeed, my (first) Pauline conversion to green buildings came about in 1973 through witnessing the knockabout act of an architect duo called Streetfarmers – so, thank you Graham Caine and Bruce Haggart for not being earnest yet having impact. Those early days included many others who became friends and who contributed significantly to my coursework and research group at Hull School of Architecture, where I was learning far more than the students. Amongst the many are: John Seymour, Peter (Jake) Chapman, Robert and Brenda Vale, Gerry Smith, Ken Yeang, Peter Schmid, Kees Duijvestein and staff and student colleagues, Michael Lloyd, Jim Low, Michael Wheeler, Ian Tod, Geoff Whittleston, Per Gustaffson, Dave Hodges, Andy McKillop, Judy Appleby, Clive Watterson and Robin Baker (at Gaia since 1993).

From the days of my professorship at Oslo (1979–82) until now, I am still learning important stuff from those students and colleagues who gave birth to Gaia Architects in 1984: Chris Butters, Frederica Miller, Dag Roalkvam, Wenche Ellingsen, Bjørn Berge, Rolf Jacobsen and Marianne Leisner. Since 1989, when Bjørn and I decided to set up Gaia International, I have been privileged to work with, and learn a whole heap from, Joachim and Barbara Eble, Rolf Messerschmidt, Declan and Margrit Kennedy, Peter Schmid, Gabriella P'al, Eva and Bruno Erat, Varis Bokalders, Paul Leech, Sally Starbuck, Kimmo and Maritta Kuismaanen, Herbert Dreiseitl, Walter Unterreiner and many more.

Most recently, I must thank Nick Grant for his shared interest in eco-minimalism; he was collecting what he called 'Limes' (green lemons) at the same time as I was collecting eco-clichés, and this process encouraged us to go into print. Meanwhile, as well as those mentioned elsewhere, Bill Bordass, Paul Woodville, Paul Jones, Barbara Chapman and John Gilbert have helped keep me from my worst rhetorical excesses with some cold, hard facts as well as good debate. At the RIAS/RIBA and in A+DS (Architecture and Design Scotland), co-founder of SEDA, Sebastian Tombs and Raymond Young (both client and friend) have given constant support and encouragement to our work.

Acknowledgements

There is, in fact, a whole book, waiting 'in the wings' to be written, about those who have been influential in the sustainable-development world over the past 40 years and earlier – many of whom I have been very privileged to meet and talk with. These include Richard Buckminster Fuller, E. F. Schumacher and, now a personal and much-respected friend, George McRobie – all of whom have inspired with their passion as much as their wise words. I am particularly grateful to George and also to Robin Harper, the UK's first Green MP, for agreeing to contribute some words for me. And a special thanks goes to Matthew Thompson of RIBA Publishing for his patience and humour and our endless games of email 'tag'. Only he and I shall ever know which words of his were slipped into the text, but I was pleased to be a party to his own modest authorship ambitions.

I owe so much to my 'partner in business and my partner in life',[3] Sandy Halliday (my second 'Pauline' conversion, since that is her middle name) that there is no start or finish. Sandy came into my life at what I aim to be its halfway stage, and transformed just about everything in it. She has been the sounding board, other half of a '365/7' dialogue and balanced critic for every thought and brainstorm idea I have had over the past 12 years – to the point where I often can't remember the individual source of many of the ideas about which I now write. For her influence on my world I am eternally grateful, and to her influence on this book I pay enormous tribute.

However, I take full and personal responsibility for any inaccuracies, errors or omissions in the script. I am sure that every reader will find something to question, and, indeed, quietly hope so – as this will mean that the text has been truly read, and that will be thanks enough for the effort expended in putting it together.

Howard Liddell
Gaia Architects, Edinburgh, 2008

3 Return quote from *Sustainable Construction* by Sandy Halliday.

Introduction

'man is far too
clever to be
able to survive
without wisdom'

E. F. Schumacher

The Glencoe Visitor Centre brief asked for the lightest eco-footprint possible, within conventional costs. The strategy was to improve the fabric and reduce the mechanical services from a norm of 30 to 9 per cent.

Gaia Architects 2003. Photo Michael Wolshover

I hope this book is timely. Otherwise, an awful lot of money is going to be wasted, in the name of sustainability, on 'eco-bling', as people technically fix their 'green' badges to their unsuspecting buildings.

If they are putting costly photovoltaic cells, hot-water solar collectors and personal wind turbines on their becalmed, north-facing, turf-roofed, toxic timber-clad, non-airtight, poorly insulated houses, finished in high-emission materials – and they are sinking electricity-powered heat pumps and rainwater-filtration systems down deep holes filled with recycled concrete, next to their reed-bed gardens with a focal-point bird table – then they could, just possibly, be spending money more wisely.

The alternative, which is both cheaper and has much better green credentials, is 'eco-minimalism' – a good-housekeeping approach to ecological building design and specification, involving apparently non-glaringly obvious strategies such as insulation, draught-proofing and the use of healthy materials. This book looks critically at a range of both the technical-fix and the good-housekeeping options that are available to the aspiring green developer – be they involved in an 'above-the-garage' bedroom extension, an 'eco-town' or a major urban masterplan project. The principles outlined here are relevant throughout all scales of building.

This book is intended to showcase an approach that represents not just good 'green' value for money, but, quite simply, good value for money.

Background

The basic motivation for this book lies in the desire to avoid a feeling of déjà vu. Many of us have been here before – anyone old enough to remember the OPEC oil-price-rise crisis of 1973 will also faintly recall the rush to all forms of alternative energy as a panacea for solving the world's problems. We raced to construct (and, fortunately, also to monitor) every device – literally – under the sun, and wind, and wave, and tide (lunar power!). In certain circumstances, some of these solutions even worked – and people were encouraged to develop them further, despite the appalling lack of funding After all, this was the realm of a few hippies and 'environmentalists'. Funny, really: we thought that everyone should have a (positive and inquisitive) interest in 'the hand that feeds us' – i.e. the environment.

For many of us, this technical pursuit was also a 'shop window' fronting a comprehensive store of healthy 'pro-planet' and yet pro-development thinking. The 'S' word – sustainability – had not yet come into play, whereas now, of course, it replaces commas in sentences and is used so often in the wrong – or oversimplistic, or one-dimensional – context. But these initial pursuits, occuring during a time of what Prime Minister Harold Wilson (along with the then Minister for Technology, Tony Benn) called the 'white heat of technology', did indeed sow the seeds of something that would evolve as a much more holistic 'tree of knowledge', and become known as sustainable development.

'those who cannot learn from history are doomed to repeat it'

George Santayana

Concorde - forged in the period of the "white heat of technology" - it was never updated as a passenger flying concept yet was still a futuristic image forty years later. Meanwhile the future was turning out differently.

Photo Khuong Hoang

'It's not personal'

St George's School, Wallasey, is the UK's earliest purpose-designed solar project. It was later monitored and compared to an equivalent neighbour school. It was found that 30 per cent of the reductions were down to the solar gains and the rest to low ventilation, the occupants and high-wattage lighting.

Architect Emslie Morgan 1965. Photo Howard Liddell

The Streetfarmers were a green direct action student architect group, who built their self-sufficient eco-house for £1,500 in the grounds of South Bank Poly and lived in it for 18 months.

Architects Streetfarmers 1974. Photo Howard Liddell

An early and simple, passive, Eco-house was built in the suburbs of Stockholm by Bengt Warne in 1977. The living quarters were on the first floor, the bedrooms and ablutions in the cellar and the garden under glass on the roof.

Architect Bengt Warne. Photo Howard Liddell

It seems that the common response to the realisation that climate change and a concern for the environment are not luxury issues is to take a global perception and then make a highly personal response. We recycle cans, bottles and paper in the office, build an eco-extension, draught-seal an existing dwelling, and so on. Maybe it is because the requisite effective action is at a level so immense that it is necessary to start with what an individual can control, i.e. their own life and behaviour. There is a basic need, born of frustration, to do SOMETHING.

However, it is in our community, professional, commercial and political activity that we can make the most impact: moving on from the 'autonomous' house to the low-impact community, and, in the case of the designing and constructing professions, to the delivery of what they design and build. The impact of an architect half-filling the office kettle is of minuscule significance set beside the specification of an airtight and highly insulated building, which will also save a lot of money for the building users and reduce its carbon footprint ('win-win').

And so it was in the 1970s (in the case of Wallasey School, the 1960s) that, looking beyond their personal behaviour, a whole raft of experimenters (with dress codes ranging from green boiler suits at the Streetfarm to Savile Row suits or brown corduroy at the Cambridge Autarkic House) built things of very varying prices and with equally varying degrees of success. But they built, and that was important, so that we could learn what worked and what didn't.

In an age of obsession with risk assessment, it is highly unlikely that half of these experimental projects would see the light of day now – and yet it is often claimed that while it is not always clear why something was successful, it is usually obvious why something failed.

Learning from the past (a 1970s House for the Future)

things should
be as simple as
possible –
but no simpler

Albert Einstein

The 1970s TV programme *A House for the Future* was a response to its contemporary political situation, which came in the wake of the OPEC action – seen at the time as an 'energy crisis'.

Inevitably, the focus of the programme was on energy and energy technology, but its demonstration building did get the basics – airtightness and high insulation levels – right, and it did also involve the very hands-on Grant family: one of the very first 'reality TV' families. In the final two programmes, it also looked at the wider picture – including the author's solar terraces project in Hull.

For a television programme, the most important aspect was that it should be visual and engage the interest of the audience. For the Grant family, and all those involved in the building, the conversion of their 'green' house (a product) into a 'sustainable' way of life (a process) was of much more significance.

Geoff Grant was very handy and technically competent, and he and his family kept very good records of the house in use. In going back to the project one year later, with some of the students who helped in the building, we learned a great deal.

In the diagram below is a list of the key eco-technologies used in the house. Over the 13 weeks of the programme, one technology per week would be the focus of attention. Highlighted in red are the ones that really worked.

Once its energy demand had been brought down, the whole house could effectively be heated by casual gains from the family, equipment, lights and – especially – by heat recovery from the kitchen. The simple lesson? To look at lowering the demand for energy in the first place before getting excited about alternative energy technology on the supply side of the equation.

Granada TV 1976 – House for the Future. The conversion of a brick barn in Macclesfield into an eco-house. The selected family got volunteer help – including from the author and Hull architecture students.

Producer Brian Trueman.
Architect Don Wilson 1976.
Photo Howard Liddell

What worked?

- High insulation levels
- Airtight skin
- Active solar roof
- Passive solar greenhouse
- Rock store under greenhouse
- Heat pump
- Wind turbine
- Heat recovery from kitchen
- Energy saving fittings
- Low emb. energy materials
- Allotment garden
  etc, etc

UK Design Award for a house that happened to be green

Back in the late 1980s, Peter and Marjorie Bourne, a Perthshire artist and teacher respectively, did not want a standard kit house but an architect-designed house. However, they wanted it on a budget not dissimilar to that of a kit house – a tall order, but that was the brief.

Any technical-fix add-ons would almost certainly have ended up being taken off at the final pre-construction budget check.

The preliminary concepts started, therefore, with a passive design approach, and the envelope had airtightness and insulation levels as high as was considered worthwhile at the time. It did eventually survive with a single 5 kW wood-burning stove heating the whole of its 160 m² floor area.

The two-storey house was designed with a south-facing (passive solar) stairwell, with four half levels, and the building was completed for a cost of £86,000 in 1992. The clients were offered twice that price for the house on the day they moved in.

In dealing with passive solar gain, the building also addressed wider lighting issues – particularly so that the clients could continue with their painting. It was also a house which they found very healthy, and they talked about the positive impact of the smell and the colour of the natural wood and breathable, mineral-paint finishes.

The project fought a few battles – actually because (a) it was not like a standard (timber-frame) kit house and (b) because it was clad in timber externally. It started on a separate site in 1989, and, owing to Planning Department resistance to it being granted permission, was finally built in the back garden of the client's former home and handed over in 1992.

In 1995, and after the house had acquired a number of awards, the local authority, who had resisted the project for nearly two years, included it in their handbook as an exemplar of how to build houses in the countryside.

Tressour Wood House for Peter and Marjorie Bourne was the UK House of the Year 1993 a Design Award for a house that happened to be green. No bells or whistles – just simple passive design.

GAIA Architects 1992.
Photo Colin Wishart

The Four Elements

to live comfortably we need to deal effectively with four elements:

Air, water, earth (materials) and fire (energy)

We humans have only been out of the caves and constructing our own habitat in the open for about 10,000 years. Termites got there well before us, and have been building for over 200 million years. Apart from controlling temperature, with earth, part of the sophistication of the termite mound is the way in which its walls 'breathe' – the way that they deal with moisture and air passively – and all this without technology, merely using intuitive, very well-applied science.

Our tendency through the 20th century was to rely increasingly on technology to deal with air and moisture in our buildings, whereas we used to allow the building fabric to cope with this. We have also come to depend ever more on technology for processed, composite and artificial building materials and for our energy supply and equipment.

My practice, GAIA, has developed an approach to design which seeks to close the loops on all these four elements (as shown opposite), in the interests of pursuing good science, before reaching for increasingly over-engineered and often inappropriate technological solutions.

A project using materials as termites and nest-builders do - for a proposed Centre for Animal Architecture.

Architect Gaia 2004. Photo & model Icosis

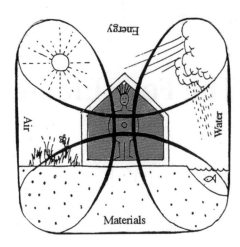

The way we came to build in the 20th century disregarded not just where goods and services came from and where they went to at the end of their usage 'cycle', but even the impact they could have on human comfort and human habitat whilst incorporated in buildings.

Image Bjørn Berge

In building for the 21st century – and with our children's health, wellbeing and future in mind – we need to take a more cyclic approach, whereby we know where we seek to resolve the cycles without environmental damage.

Image Bjørn Berge

**'Where is it from?
How is it used?
Where does it go?'**

Instead of having a linear flow of the four elements, we seek to have a cyclic flow. This is about knowing where something comes from, knowing how to use it well – in other words, using it to its maximum potential – and knowing where it will go to at the end of its functional life.

Just as this construct has been used successfully in ecological building design, so it has been used as an organising principle for the two core chapters of this book.

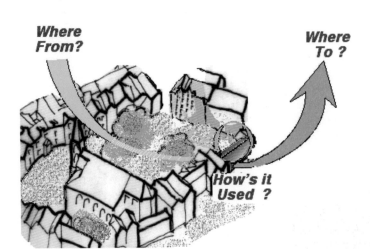

In working with groups of 10-year-olds on their utopian eco-cities we have developed a simple set of rules. They need to know where the four elements for their buildings come from, where they go to at the end of their useful life and how they work when incorporated into buildings.

Image Howard Liddell

"the system of nature, of which man is a part, tends to be self-balancing, self-adjusting, self-cleansing, not so with technology."

E. F. Schumacher

technical fix

Tuscan Sunrise. Photo Howard Liddell

fire

/ Photovoltaic Solar Cells
/ Heat Pumps
/ CHP (Combined Heat and Power)
/ Thermal Solar Collector
/ Condensing Boilers
/ District Heating

element

Photovoltaic Solar Cells:
An expensive way to use the sun?

The triumphant power of electricity and its attendant gadgetry to 'free the housewife from drudgery' – which, in the 1920s and 30s, it did indeed do – has created a love affair with all things electrical; it was the 20th century's 'sexy' energy supply.

Since the advent of the solar-powered calculator, there has been an optimistic industry developing an optimistic body of potential customers transfixed by the promise of electrical power from the sun through photovoltaic solar cells.

But electricity generation has always had a major drawback – it is bound to be more expensive than the oil, coal, gas and nuclear sources that, predominantly, it exploits for its creation by comparison with using those same fuels directly. In other words, the direct energy from burning oil, for example, will always be cheaper than the cost of electricity generated from burning oil. Solar-energy supply to a consumer is no different: like any basic fuel, it is only as cheap as the cost of exploiting it for an end use.

In the case of photovoltaic cells, the hope has always been that the exploitation cost would drop rapidly with increase in demand, and that economies of scale would kick in. However, at the point of writing this seems as far away as the economic delivery of nuclear fusion that was once promised as 'too cheap to meter' – or, indeed, the tantalising (but unrealised) promise in the 1950s of the abundance of nuclear fission.

At present, very large areas of PV cells are required for meaningful levels of energy output. The payback period for this technology is, at best, 50 years. In addition, we need to bear in mind that, in use, it reduces in efficiency by about 1 per cent each year. At about £25,000, the price of a 5 kW solar array could buy an awful lot of more cost-effective strategies – not least, insulation and airtight construction.

photovoltaics seem almost magic – they turn sunlight into electricity.

but it takes rather a lot of photovoltaic cells to make not very much electricity.

This top floor of an otherwise (primarily) passive and low carbon 4-storey block of academic offices has 34kw of photovoltaics feeding a building where the all-glazed room itself has a heating demand greater then 34kw. The array has also failed after 3 years and requires total replacement.

ZICER building, VEA. Photo Howard Liddell

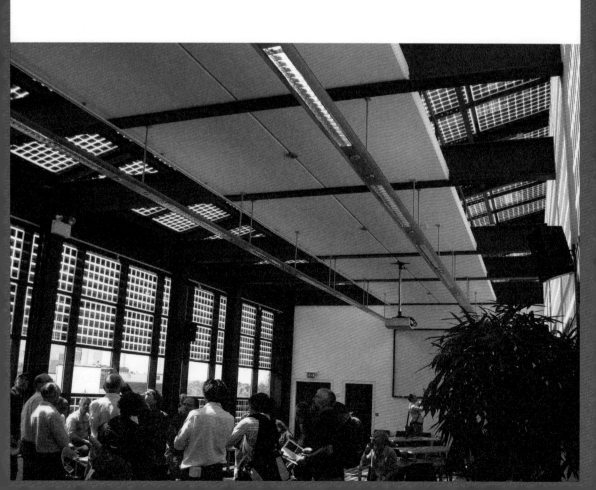

Heat Pumps:
Do they beat the gas/ electricity cost difference?

Heat pumps are often the energy technology of first choice for the green client and are much vaunted by those sold on the marketing spin, which promises as much as four to five energy units out for only one put in.

A heat pump (like that at the core of most modern fridges, for example) exploits the property of certain 'phase-change' chemicals to extract or expel heat as they convert from liquid to gas (and produce freezing conditions at the other side of the system in the process – hence, the fridge). The gas is then repeatedly compressed back to a liquid by a compressing pump driven by electrical energy.

However, electricity costs more than other fuels per unit of energy output because it is a secondary source of energy supply, produced from a primary fuel (most commonly oil, coal or gas). To make a direct comparison, the example of a power station that creates electricity using gas is being considered here. Such power stations historically have been unable to exploit the gas at more than 40 per cent efficiency, and averaged out over time their performance has been much lower than this. 'Grid losses' (i.e. the energy lost in transmitting the electricity from power stations along cables to the end-user) run at about 8 per cent, and when these are added it is clear that electricity in our homes is delivered very inefficiently when referring back to the primary fuel from which it is derived – in this case, gas.

The differential in tariffs between one unit of gas and one equivalent unit of electricity is around three to one. Given that this is about the same as the average output efficiency of a heat pump – i.e. about three units out to one unit in (based on the author's experience of three separate installations as monitored, rather than as marketed) – it seems like an awful lot of technical complication, expense and effort to get back to where we started. One unit of gas, which could have been used directly in the first instance in a 97 per cent efficient domestic condensing boiler, arrives instead in a heat-pump supply system as derived energy from a long journey – via a rank of industrial gas boilers, a hall of turbines, miles and miles of national grid and, finally, a domestic heat pump as one-quarter to one-third of a unit of electricity.

Taking the argument away from mere cost and on to carbon footprint, heat pumps can make sense but only if there is a direct connection to the heat pump from a renewable supply such as a wind turbine. In this case, the carbon figure at least becomes positive. However, in the UK – for the foreseeable future – any cost benefits will remain out of reach.

the equipment: one energy unit in – three units out.

the energy supply: electricity costs three times as much as the gas that generated it.

result: an exercise in technological redundancy.

Most houses have a version of a heat pump – at the back of the fridge. It uses freon which absorbs heat (from food and drink) when changing phase from liquid to gas. The heat is then rejected as the pump compresses the gas back to liquid.

Photo Howard Liddell

CHP (Combined Heat and Power):
Balancing hot water and electricity.

Hot air emerging from a power station's cooling towers seems such a waste. To exploit the waste heat and use it for making hot water appears, clearly, to be a better option. However, it is how this secondary exploitation can be used that presents the challenge. Whilst the demand for electricity and for domestic hot water is relatively constant, the round-the-year demand for hot water for space heating is not. The only way this can work efficiently is if the hot-water requirement of the total system is constant (e.g. round-the-clock and year-round, such as for a hospital or swimming pool).

In most situations, the overall summer hot-water demand of a building will be significantly lower than its overall winter hot-water demand. Therefore, if the system has been sized for the maximum loading (in winter), then the hot water coming from the electricity-generation process in the summer will need to have somewhere other than a space-heating network to go to – or be jettisoned (e.g. as in a cooling tower).

The other option is to have a CHP system sized on the summer load only, and have an additional system for supplying the extra winter demand. This does, however, mean the installation of two systems rather than one, which will then reduce much of the basic benefit.

There has been much research over the past 30 years into alternative ways of generating electricity that would overcome the above dilemma – such as the (solar-powered) Stirling cycle engine – but, as yet, there is little in the form of applied output.

using the waste heat from electricity
generation for hot water only works
with a constant round-the-year
demand for hot water.

The CHP plant black building
at Loretto, Tübingen, sits next
to the parking machine building
and is powered by
gas and biofuel.

Architects Tübingen City Council.
Photo Howard Liddell

Thermal Solar Collector:
Will it last long enough to pay for itself?

This is possibly the oldest 'green badge' technology. Customers often want an obvious outward demonstration of their green intentions, and this shouts it from the rooftops (even if it doesn't move like a wind turbine!).

The thermal solar collector, which basically seeks to heat water directly from the sun, is probably the oldest and simplest of all the eco-technologies. If kept simple and if self-built, it can be very cost-effective. For example, a second-hand radiator painted black with an underlying insulating layer and a sheet of glass over it will heat water from the sun's rays reasonably effectively. If an off-the-peg commercial installation is purchased, then it is likely to be less easy to justify on cost terms.

Most of the first generation of commercial solar-thermal installations worked technically but not constructionally, and many have not survived long enough to pay back their investment. In the UK – depending on location – this payback period (the length of time it takes for the capital cost of the equipment to match the value of the energy obtained over time from the sun) is usually quoted at around 12 to 15 years.

A paradox exists, whereby the more one pays for the quality of the solar-thermal apparatus, the longer the payback period. This is because there is insufficient difference in energy-efficiency between a simple home-made collector and a sophisticated top-of-the-range commercial product.

in the right place, at the right angle, it will work best on sunny days, and inefficiently on overcast days.

how long is the payback time?

The Centre for Alternative Technology in Wales has been testing out industry-produced thermal solar collectors since 1973. In terms of cost -efficiency (payback period), none can come close to their home-made versions.

Home made solar collector. AT. Photo Howard Liddell

Condensing Boilers:
Cheap ones don't condense.

Condensing boilers have already been enshrined in the good-practice manuals and are generally regarded as a 'good thing'. Given the relatively small difference in cost between a non-condensing boiler and a condensing unit it seems a perfectly logical choice, and, indeed, in most cases is probably good practice.

Basically, the condensing boiler is designed to burn its gas fuel more efficiently and to give off fewer emissions from the flue. Such a technical provision certainly scores well in government-backed rating schemes such as the 'SAP' ratings required by the Building Regulations, and as a score for BREEAM[4] building assessments. However, cheap units can fail very quickly, and unless people invest in quality, they will find that they have merely participated in a cynical 'tick the green box' exercise. After a couple of years, they can end up being no better off than they would be with a conventional boiler.

The *context* of the installation is also important. Is the building fabric – in its walls, floors and ceilings – energy-efficient in the first place? Is there a high level of insulation, and is the building airtight? These issues are important because if the building is constructed to minimum standards (or built below them, as is all too often the case), then the main benefit of a condensing boiler is already lost – and more.

It is also worth having the demand side calculated, since the methods used by many heating installers are rudimentary and often based merely on gross square metreage, irrespective of the energy-efficiency of the building envelope. As installers will want to guarantee thermal performance, their estimate will always tend towards the worst-case scenario – and this will doubly penalise energy-efficient homeowners. In the first instance, they will be paying for boilers larger than they need, and, secondly, the units will always be operating at a lower output than is efficient, since boilers work most efficiently when going flat out.

4 Building Research Establishment Environmental Assessment Method.

cheap boilers often fail
to condense after a
short period.
oversized installations will
always operate inefficiently.

The author has had disappointing
experience with condensing
boilers, and has learnt that cheap
ones often fail within months.

Photo Howard Liddell

District Heating:
Specific to context, layout and form.

The reasoning behind district heating is that having many buildings connected to a centralised delivery system will produce efficiencies, economies of scale and reduced costs for heating. One central-heating boiler system is traded off in cost terms against lots of small individual ones in each building.

The critical issues then become:

> the overall layout of the buildings being supplied (from low-rise, low-density suburbia to high-rise, high-density inner-city buildings)

> the energy-efficiency of the individual properties being supplied (and rewards for the most efficient)

> the distance that the hot water in the flow and return pipes needs to travel between properties.

Clearly, the denser a development, the more efficient it will tend to be; therein lies the critical point that precedes any decision-making on such a technology. However, with the privatisation of the energy-supply industry and the associated individual rights to change supplier, the consistency over time of the demand, and therefore the long-term viability of such an installation, can look risky.

the intention is efficiency through economies of scale.

the demand needs to be consistent and the distances short for this to be delivered.

In the small and compact village of Blons in a Vorarlberg forest, this woodchip plant feeds all the main community buildings and a significant number of the neighbouring houses. It works here because of the compactness of the village and readily available woodchip.

Photo Howard Liddell

air

/ Conservatories
/ Small Wind Turbines
/ Mechanical Ventilation

element

Conservatories:
90 per cent have heating in them.

Conservatories are assumed to be an all-round 'good thing' from an energy point of view. It is for this reason that they can be built without the need for Planning or Building Regulation permissions for all locations barring Conservation Areas.

However, any positive benefits – a reduction in wind-chill on the external wall against which the conservatory is placed, and free passive solar gains coming through the glass – are of no value if the conservatory is then fitted with a heating system. Any heating system placed in a conservatory will spend most of its energy heating the sky on the other side of the very high heat-loss glass (even if it is double- or triple-glazed). If the heating appliances are connected to the house central-heating system and are not separately zoned, then this already negative situation is exacerbated.

This is a case of the triumph of sociology over technology. People want to be in their glazed spaces in midwinter, and not just on sunny days. A recent survey[5] established that 90 per cent of conservatories have some form of heating system in them. This converts a carbon-saving strategy into a carbon-using one.

Slightly less significant – but still of note – is the fact that there is quite a lot of embodied energy in the glass and the supporting structure of a conservatory. For the first few years of its life (even if it is unheated), the carbon saving delivered by the greenhouse effect will be paying off the energy used in the structure's manufacture and delivery to site.

conservatories were exempted from planning permission on the basis that they would make a positive energy contribution to houses. the reality is the exact opposite.

5 Professor Tadj
Oreszczyn, Lecture
on Energy Efficiency
at Royal Institution,
Glasgow,
15 February 2006.

This 1980s Perthshire Conservatory by GAIA has now been fitted out with a jacuzzi and underfloor heating. Not a cheap decision, for the client or the planet.

Gaia Architects 1995. Photo Howard Liddell

Small wind Turbines:
Wind turbines need to be where the wind is.

The significant and powerful lobby against 'wind turbines on the hill' insists, somewhat disingenuously, that it is not against wind power per se – merely the large wind farms that make a visible impact on the landscape, (although it is not usually mentioned that these areas are often already disfigured by geometric patches of heather burning). This argument has influenced the move to small wind turbines, taking them off the hills and instead onto buildings – a strategy exacerbated by policies such as the 'Merton Rule' (which demands a level of 10 per cent on-site renewables). However, the relative cost-effectiveness, efficiency, energy output and even carbon footprint of the two options is very different. A recent study for a 14-house development in Cornwall demonstrated a twofold increase in the capital cost of investing in small-scale as opposed to large-scale turbines, and an increase of a factor of 20 in the energy output by large-scale rather than small-scale turbines.[6]

We should learn from the wind-turbine-manufacturing industry in Germany, which has become discredited for selling grant-assisted small-scale turbines to householders in becalmed areas, who, not unreasonably, have been very unhappy with the performance of their (albeit subsidised) investments. Effective wind-exploitation opportunities are very location-specific, and a blanket policy of removing the need for planning permission for small turbines will both be ineffective and rapidly bring wind power into disrepute.

Any discussion of micro-installations is always about grid connection (or not). It is feasible to use wind energy for purposes other than feeding into a 240-volt interface with the national grid – it can go to battery storage, with output into 12- or 24-volt systems or to a heat churn (making hot water through friction from blades attached to a turbine). Alternatively, it can be used to pump water or for some other mechanical, rather than electrical, purpose.

6 Source: Peter
Warm Associates.

as builders throughout the centuries have tended to place houses in sheltered locations, it is unlikely that many houses are sitting on a prime wind-turbine site.

Amongst nine highly different experimental houses in Skive, Denmark, this wind-powered version had a heat churn system (for creating hot water). It lasted mere days when the vibrations were found to be excessive.

Various architects 1977. Photo Howard Liddell

Mechanical Ventilation:
Absorptive materials before extract fans.

If you find yourself having to get away quickly but needing an unavoidable visit to the WC, the post-event hand-washing decision is easy. On the wall there is an automatic 7 kW electrically powered hand-dryer, and next to it a paper towel dispenser. Not only will the paper towel do the job more quickly, it will do it more cheaply, will use orders of magnitude less carbon and, if the sign by the electrical hand-dryer in a certain City Council Department of Environmental Health is to be believed, it is also '250 times more hygienic' than using the hand-dryer.

Fans are reasonably efficient at moving air around, but not very effective at dealing with moisture. There is a very interesting development amongst ecological-design architects, who are using materials that are 'vapour open'. These include untreated timber (especially end grain) hemp/lime and unbaked clay, in either plaster or brick form. When these are left natural – or are treated with mineral paints, which are also 'vapour open' (i.e. moisture transfusive) – the ventilation requirement for mitigating humidity is dramatically reduced. There is much anecdotal evidence of mirrors not steaming up in bathrooms in which such materials are used, as the walls are acting as a moisture buffer and ironing out the peaks and troughs.

My experience is that mechanical services engineers do not accept hygroscopicity as a relevant factor and will over specify the ventilation system accordingly.

7 DTU (2005) *Moisture Buffering of Building Materials:*
Report BYG°EDTU R-126 from the Department of Civil
Engineering, Technical University of Denmark.

finnish research has shown that hygroscopic (moisture-absorbing) materials are nine times more effective than mechanical ventilation at dealing with indoor humidity.

This kitchen extract system from a brand new BREEAM Excellent – rated building in Scotland makes the author think that the engineers may have taken the (equipment-industry-written) CIBSE Specification Guide too much to heart.

Photo Howard Liddell

earth

element

Green Roofs:
Do they merely camouflage the dodgy environmental credentials of what lies underneath?

The expression 'turf roof' has become a generic term that covers a whole range of different types of planted roof surfaces. Often the term 'green roof' is used instead. The original Norwegian vernacular tradition involved 30 to 40 cm of earth being thrown up onto a roof covered with 28 layers of birch bark for waterproofing.

In modern construction, such a strategy of a (literal) earth or turf roof usually depends for its existence on a petrochemical-based damp-proofing membrane and extra structural support. Neither of these elements readily comes to mind as environmentally sound specification

There are now a number of patent sedum roof systems, all of which appear to avoid the weight and some of the material problems, and they justify themselves (a) as solar screening for a flat roof membrane and (b) as part of a SUDS strategy for retaining water from the watercourses. However, they often merely camouflage a traditional asphalt roof, and their longevity is yet to be proven.

All of the above lays aside aesthetic considerations as to whether turf roofs belie an attitude that any form of human construction is an affront to a natural setting, and that therefore camouflage is a preferable option to a loud-and-proud architecture.

the phenomenon of the turf roof is probably at least one of the images preventing architects – unaware that ecological design is an approach and not a style – from 'going green': they constitute another superfluous clip-on badge for the undiscerning architectural student, innocent of their 'hobbitland' aesthetic.

A turf roof is usually heavy and camouflaging a plastic membrane. A sedum option does at least reduce the additional roof load, but still has the look of Middle Earth about it.

Jane Darbyshire & David Kendall Ltd. Photo Howard Liddell

Recycled Materials:
Last in the hierarchy of reuse, renew, recycle.

Recycling – commonly a 'catch-all' phrase covering reuse, renewal and recycling – is often one of the first things that a new convert to the green agenda thinks about.

The associated word 'recyclable' is bandied about as if it really meant something. However, is not everything on earth recyclable somehow? (The author has a bottle of whisky for the first person to send in a suggestion of a material or product that cannot be recycled in some form – even plutonium gets recycled!)

The question is one of how easy and safe it is to recycle a material. Some are relatively simple and others near-impossible – especially at affordable prices. It is very easy to establish whether a building has been constructed with recycling in mind in the first place. There are a couple of structures in central London built with innovative 1960s methods that have become causes célèbres, as they are considered virtually impossible to demolish without spraying half of the capital with (post-tensioned) concrete. Knowing what we know now, nobody in their right mind would invent reinforced concrete as an easily recyclable material. Its demolition is extremely time- and cost-intensive.

Doing it differently, and in particular cheaply and safely, is a design challenge that the author would like to throw at the industry.

recycling is the last resort, because it virtually
always requires significant processing
and inputs of additional resources in order
to transform the recycled material into
something both benign and useful.

In observing the dismantling of a not very old flyover, it becomes clear that it was never ever intended to be taken apart, otherwise why would it take so long and be so difficult to take down?

Oslo ex-motorway. Photo Howard Liddell

Local Materials:
Unstitching a globalised world is no small challenge, but is it actually an environmentally sound strategy – or mere nostalgia?

In an age of globalisation there is something quaint about the notion of returning to local materials and to local labour.

The assumption is that using local materials is inevitably going to be cheaper because they have not come as far as an imported material, and they will also have reduced embodied energy because they won't have been transported as far. In addition, the process keeps money in the local economy, and that is a socio-economic sustainability issue. However, the reality of pursuing this goal in a world wedded to both certification and centralisation means that a whole raft of institutional hurdles tend to undermine it, and it is even, ironically, vulnerable to misplaced opportunism by local people.

For example, UK timber with a relatively low structural grading might (a) need to be installed using much larger volumes of wood, (b) still need to be taken many miles away from its woodland for stress-grading before being returned to its nearby site, and (c) have poor weathering properties.

what if you live in glasgow and your most
abundant local product is a pvc window?

what if a client decides to go for a local architect
who has no experience of using local materials?

Not everyone is as fortunate
as the residents of the
Grenoble region, who can dig
up – from right under their
feet – the perfect raw material
for their buildings with just
the right amount of sand
content for earth building.

Various architects – Domaine de
la Terre, Ile d'Abeau, 1993.
Photo Howard Liddell

Timber Cladding:
Where does it come from? How has it been treated?

Many architects acknowledge that timber cladding is the first material they think of when being asked to design an environmentally sound building. However, if it is from an unidentified source, or one that makes unverifiable claims to be sustainable (as is the case with a huge amount of tropical hardwood), then it is very questionable whether its pedigree would stand up to scrutiny in terms of a global strategy for sustainable forestry.

On the other hand, if it is a cheap form of timber it will usually be treated – and the ubiquitous treatments, mostly based on CCA (chromated copper arsenic), are decidedly not environmentally friendly. Indeed, the timbers become potential toxic waste from the moment they are treated, thereby causing an end-of-useful-life disposal problem.

Any non-porous surface treatment to timber cladding – such as petrochemical paint or polyurethane varnish – will also prevent the wood from breathing and cause worse weathering and maintenance problems than it would have had if it had been left alone.

like turf roofs, timber cladding is a 'camouflage' material often used by aspiring green architects with a limited understanding of the issues.

The Austrians love their timber to weather and go black in places. However, they do not do this without attention to longevity: it is merely their taste – not shared by northern Europeans. In the UK such a vision is likely to be the result of poor timber choice.

School in Vorarlberg. Photo Howard Liddell

water

/ Reed Beds
/ Grey-water Recycling
/ 'Living Machines'
/ Rainwater Harvesting

element

Water sculpture, Asperg by Herbert Dreiseitl.
Photo Howard Liddell

Reed Beds:
Context-dependent.

A favourite of architecture students trying to assert their green credentials, the reed bed sits alongside the solar collector and the building-mounted wind turbine as a highly visible green badge, and is part of the ubiquitous 'green box' of clip-on 'eco-bling'.

Where there is an abundance of land and no prospect of connecting to an existing sewerage system, then occasionally a reed-bed system (or, more usefully, a 'designed wetland') will be appropriate. It makes no sense – not even environmental sense – in an urban context with an adjacent sewerage infrastructure and capacity for the outfall.

It should be borne in mind that a reed bed is a form of monoculture (one type of reed) and that it serves primarily to bring aeration to a plant root-zone. It usually makes more sense when secondary treatment (e.g. that required after processing in a septic tank) is justified for the system to comprise a range of plants with the capacity to 'fix' or take out different toxins (e.g. heavy metals).

The land requirement for 'black' (solid-effluent) sewage treatment is anywhere between 1 and 2.5 m^2 per person, which, even at average densities, adds up quite quickly to a large area. Alternative and less land-intensive, even more environmentally sound, options are available, and each circumstance needs to be dealt with in its own right.

reed beds are land-hungry,
and do not present
themselves as a first option in
an urban context.

**This reed bed copes with the
grey water from a school. It has
an educational value beyond its
cost viability.**

Architects Kent CC.
Brenzett Primary School Kent.
Photo Sandy Halliday

Grey-water Recycling:
Who looks after it, and what does it cost?

It seems quite sensible to replace the conventional mains supply of potable-quality water to flush thirsty WC cisterns with recycled grey water. On the other hand, in areas where constancy of water supply is not a big issue it may appear an excessive capital expenditure to install secondary plumbing systems alongside the primary systems when this is set against other environmental-specification items that are competing for attention on limited budgets.

If this water is relatively uncontaminated, containing merely a small proportion of soapy deposits, then recycling it seems like an acceptable water conservation strategy. However, if biological pollution such as urine gets into the system it will require fundamental cleaning, which at the very least is likely to be expensive and inconvenient. Perfectly reasonable technical solutions are often rendered unacceptable in the face of sociological circumstances.

recycling shower and wash-hand basin water might not withstand anti-social habits.

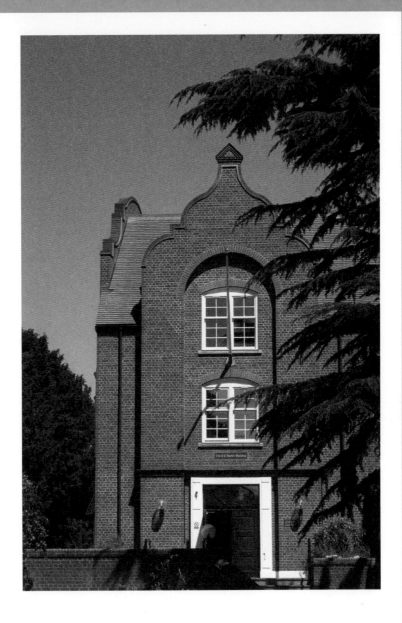

The grey water recycling in this Oxford College was switched off after just a short time when biological impurities were found coming from the student showers, baths and wash-hand basins.

Linacre College ECD Architects. Photo Henrietta Temple

'Living Machines':
Trading a sewage problem for an energy problem.

There are many municipal sewerage infrastructure systems that are over-capacity to the extent that they prevent further development in their area. In such situations, natural sewerage systems such as reed beds and 'living machines' are often being proposed, and sometimes also implemented in order to allow development to go ahead.

The so-called living machine is the brainchild of John Todd, an American water engineer, and is based on quite sophisticated and intensive aquaculture as a means of treating sewage. Unlike the reed bed, it does not take up a lot of land: it comprises a pumped system that treats water in a sequence of beds with a variety of plants, each 'fixing' or taking out different pollutants.

Whilst such a system has proven technically successful in cleaning the water, it does rely on a significant amount of input energy to run the pumps. In the case of one small community system in Scotland this expenditure runs to about £500 per week. It has been commented that this is merely trading one environmental problem, sewage, for another: energy.

'You pays your money and you takes your choice'

Anonymous

the attraction of a 'livingmachine' sewerage system is that, unlike reed-bed systems, it is land-efficient. it is, however, relatively energy-intensive.

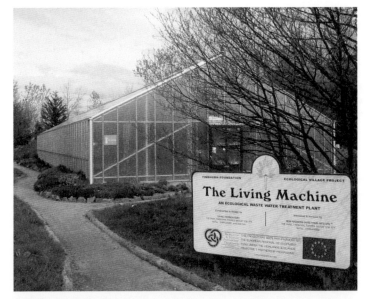

The Living Machine is an intensive self-sufficient sewage treatment plant. The one illustrated has worked well for a large community in Scotland for two decades. Its environmental credentials are sound apart from one fatal flaw – the high energy cost of pumping the system round.

Findhorn Foundation.
Photo Howard Liddell

Rainwater Harvesting:
In competing with more economical environmental strategies, this is usually a low priority.

The usual reason for harvesting rainwater at a local, site scale is to replace highly processed, potable mains water, much of which is simply used for WC flushing, with something that has not been expensively prepared for human consumption but is nonetheless perfectly adequate for the job.

Again, as with many of these new technologies, the main deterrent to its use is how much the idea costs to exploit. Most such systems need to run in parallel with the conventional system, and therefore there is a duplication in the cold-water pipework and end fittings. This is bound to involve additional expense, although there can be economies of scale in larger arrangements.

However, not all rainwater needs to be for consumption indoors, and there is a lot of scope for irrigational or ground-watering use – and even potential savings in a 'pipe-free' SUDS context. (SUDS, or Sustainable Drainage Systems, are designed to reduce urban flooding, enhance local water quality, hold rainwater for amenity purposes or encourage local wildlife, and top up groundwater.)

at root all water supplies are rainwater catchments – each site will have its own economies of scale.

Like anything else that seems to be free, rainwater is only as inexpensive to use as the exploitation costs. The cost of a rainwater barrel is relatively low – use in gardens and simple irrigation avoids the costs of filtering and dual plumbing systems.

Photo Howard Liddell

'in technology
reality must take
precedence over
public relations,
because nature
won't be fooled.'

Richard Feynmann

ecominimalism

Tuscan Sunflowers. Photo Howard Liddell.

fire

/ Passive Solar Energy
/ Solar Shading
/ Low-energy Equipment
/ Phantom Loads
/ Renewable Tariffs
/ Minimum Boilers
/ Passive House Standard

element

Passive Solar Energy:
Fewer moving parts to go wrong.

Pointing south-facing glazing at the sun and letting it heat up something solid and heat-retaining, like a tiled floor or a brick wall, is a phenomenon that will simply happen sunny-day-in and sunny-day-out, without wear and tear. Unlike an 'active' solar-energy system, passive solar design requires no plumbing or pumps and virtually no maintenance.

It is not magic, and while the 'greenhouse effect' exploited by greenhouses and conservatories means that short-wave radiation goes in and re-radiated long-wave radiation finds it difficult to get out, other forms of heat transfer – conduction (through a material), convection (in the air) and even a degree of radiation (across a space) – all contribute (once the sun has gone down) to a potential for glazing to be a net loser of energy instead of a net winner. Such losses are relatively easy to resolve via shutters or curtains, but this issue does emphasise that with a passive solar strategy the user – not the system – is active, while in an active system the opposite is the case.

the key to exploiting solar gain is to ensure that it has somewhere useful to go and is not a nuisance.

At Ile d'Abeau in France the earth construction acts as a very effective thermal store that is heated as the sun shines through the conservatory. This keeps the structure at an even temperature 24 hours a day.

Architects various. Domaine de la Terre, 1993. Photo Howard Liddell

Solar Shading:
Essential if a benefit is not to become a real nuisance.

Pointing south-facing glazing at the sun is fine for heating a building in the heating season, but such a strategy becomes a liability in the summer. Unless external shading or super-ventilation is included in the design, it is likely that there will be overheating and a resultant cooling requirement – such as air-conditioning.

Post-rationalisation of past designs often seeks to ascribe to a ubiquitous 'modern'-materials palette virtues that might not stand up to scientific scrutiny. Unfortunately, once the sun is through the glass it contributes to the building's greenhouse effect. Internal blinds merely prevent glare and visual discomfort – they do nothing to mitigate heat build-up. Therefore, it is essential that a summer cooling strategy includes external shading – for example through external blinds or brise-soleil.

Solar shading, in the form of brise-soleil, is often applied as mere decoration, adding interest to an otherwise unpromising façade without doing the job it is designed to perform. Such devices feature occasionally even on north elevations, where – certainly in the UK – their contribution to indoor climate control is zero.

the glass-and-steel dream beloved of modern architects presents a major carbon challenge.

In most circumstances other than in conservatories, the sun can be as much of a problem as an opportunity. It is essential, therefore, to have (external) shading to prevent any unwanted solar gain getting through the glazing.

Ludesch Town Centre.
Photo Howard Liddell

Low-energy Equipment:
Start by demanding less energy.

When the Chinese government decided in the late 1970s to supply its whole population with fridges, its less energy-efficient choice of model – made on a marginal capital-cost-saving basis – resulted in the electricity-supply industry having to build a significant number of additional power stations to cope with the extra load.[8] The choice appears especially strange when one considers the lack of a free market at that time. The option was there to buy a 'job lot' of a specification to the benefit not just of the state but of all comrades.

Energy rating is one of the few areas in which the EU has successfully implemented an energy-labelling and savings strategy. As this publication goes to print, the UK government has finally decided that phasing out high-energy-use light bulbs will not result in the collapse of the consumerist economy – and might even help it.

In the meantime, it virtually always makes cost-in-use sense to buy energy-efficient appliances, and while clockwork radios and torches may seem oddball, they never require a trip to the shops for spare batteries – merely a modicum of human exercise.

8 Walt Patterson, The Energy Alternative: changing the way the world works, available on http://www.waltpatterson.org/contents.htm

reducing the demand for electricity by using low-energy equipment is often caricatured as reducing our standard of living. the opposite is actually true – it will give better value for money.

As long as low energy-equipment is optional (and usually ugly too), it is unlikely to attract any but the committed greens. Time for legislation here, and a lot more commitment and effort on the part of lighting designers.

Photo Howard Liddell

Phantom Loads:

There are numerous, unnecessary, 'phantom' loads making demands on the electricity supply system.

The introduction of low-energy equipment and dealing effectively with inefficient standby modes can be achieved without threatening personal or corporate standards of living. All that's lacking is the political will to phase in the 'one-watt standby'.

Around 10 per cent of the national electricity grid and 1 per cent of the nation's total energy demand is accounted for by the standby buttons on our electrical and electronic equipment. What is remarkable is that one-watt standby is achievable with currently available technology. Indeed, there is a whole movement seeking to promote such a shift.[9] What is even more significant is that, as with digital television, it could easily be phased in over a very short period as people replaced their equipment. One-watt standby could certainly be achieved in less time than it takes to construct the nuclear power station required to cope with the utterly unnecessary waste caused by inaction on this possibility.

In Australia in 2005, an announcement was made of a strategy for the implementation of a 'One Watt' standby target for appliances, with the potential to save the average household up to AUS$100 per annum and significantly reduce greenhouse-gas emissions.

Given that this is an obvious 'win-win' solution, it seems very odd that a strategy to implement such a switch to low-energy standby electronic apparatus is taking so long to introduce to the UK. Because of not having to construct more generating capacity, there is a reduction in the expense of running additional power to the benefit of all.

While everyone argues about which form of energy is the best for the future – and that the need is urgent – there is a permanent winning card sitting in our hand that we choose not to play. We could very quickly develop across the board one-watt standby equipment instead of leaving the lights on and having to build new generating capacity.

Photo Howard Liddell

equipment sitting on 'standby' mode commands between 8 and 15 per cent of the national electricity grid's demand (estimates vary).

Renewable Tariffs:
Defraying the carbon cost of essential electricity.

It is common for clients wishing to 'go green' to look to a domestic-scale solution rather than connecting to a networked system. In generating their own energy, they take both the capital expenditure and the ongoing maintenance on board.

However, each case needs to be taken on its merit. For example, a house-mounted wind turbine is likely, in most locations, to be considerably more expensive per watt generated than a larger, more appropriately sited wind turbine. It will also generate less output per money or carbon unit invested. It will therefore probably have a larger environmental footprint than connection to a network that is exploiting wind where the wind blows rather than in a more sheltered, built-up area.

Every site is different and has its own most appropriate renewable energy source. However, very few plots are capable of efficiently sourcing their own total energy requirement either on-site or close to it. In this circumstance, the option is open either to look to a more appropriate technology or to buy into a renewables tariff from a supplier who already has a low-carbon grid supply network.

A recent client, when informed that a city-centre site was poor for exploiting wind energy, elected to buy into a turbine 100 miles away. Such a direct link was considered necessary within their carbon-neutral marketing strategy.

if a remote source of renewable energy is more carbon-efficient and more environmentally sound in the total calculation than building-mounted renewable apparatuses, does it matter how far away it is?

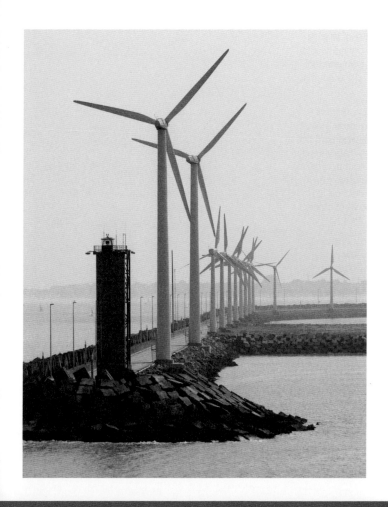

A recent report investigating a large number of microrenewable sites has indicated that they are working on average at under 8% capacity. If we are to use renewables we must use them efficiently and that will often mean at large scale and centralised.

Photo Zeebruge, Howard Liddell

Minimum Boilers:

There is an unmet need for low-output boilers for low-energy housing.

Until recently, domestic boiler installations have been oversized for use in energy-efficient houses, and therefore have been working inefficiently. Given that boilers work most efficiently when operating at full load and inefficiently when on reduced load, there is a clear wastage in both the additional cost of the redundant installed capacity and the economic operation of such systems. It has only recently become possible to obtain high-ratio turn-down boilers (up to 4:1 turn-down), which arrangement allows them to work efficiently at both high output (say, 16 kW) and low output (say, 4 kW).

With the advent of ever-increasing numbers of energy-efficient homes, the further development of purely low-output condensing boilers is to be welcomed (with the caveat of comments made under the section on 'Condensing Boilers' and their quality – see pp. 25-26).

as energy-performance standards increase, the need for large-scale boilers will diminish and, at domestic scale, we will be looking for less-than-5 kw boilers as the norm.

It is only recently that boilers of a sufficient 'turn-down' ratio have become available. In energy-efficient homes large boilers will never be able to work flat out and therefore efficiently.

Variable output woodstove in Austrian house.
Photo Sandy Halliday

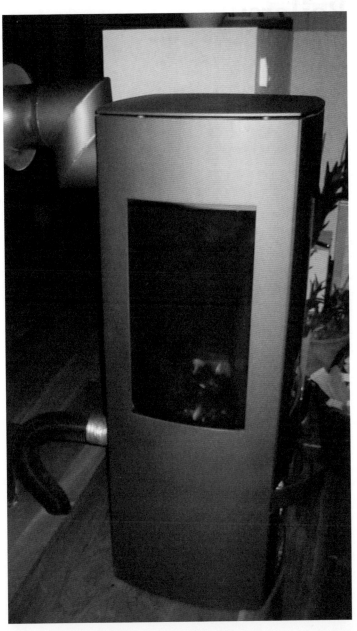

Passive House Standard:

There is no such thing as a zero-energy building, but there can be a zero-space-heating building.

The 'passive house standard' is defined as a standard of dwelling that not only does not require any heating system but also cools down by no more than half a degree Celsius over 12 hours. This might seem quite stringent, but such houses have been built in central Europe, Scandinavia and Canada for years.

There is a debate about the extent of the (electricity) demand required by the heat-recovery systems that are usually specified in order to avoid heat loss in the extract ventilation air. However, this is an 'advanced-class' discussion in the context of the poor insulation and airtightness standards currently prevalent in buildings being constructed the UK.

New clients very rarely approach our architect's practice asking for a passive house; it is, however, very common for them to have a strong opinion about supply-side technology – be that a heat pump, a wind turbine, a solar collector or a biomass boiler. The possibility that none of these might be necessary in the first place is currently not even part of the public debate.

labelling schemes, such as the code for sustainable homes, are having an impact on moving a proportion of new buildings towards the passive house standard

In this row of terraced houses in Austria, the central houses have no heating system and maintain a temperature 24/7 and 365 days per year above 22°C.

Butschens, Austria. Architect W. Unterreiner.
Photo Howard Liddell

Balloon regatta in France. Photo Howard Liddell

element

Airtightness:
Build tight and ventilate right.

It is still the case that the purpose of airtight construction is misunderstood by many who are concerned about its health impacts. An airtight unventilated building does indeed have negative health impacts on its occupants; some air movement is absolutely essential, but the ventilation rate must be controllable and therefore independent of the outdoor wind regime. This is clearly not the case in draughty buildings, but a properly designed airtight building can maintain a consistent ventilation rate in any wind. It is the control and consistency that are important. The mantra is 'build tight and ventilate right'.

Super-insulation

It only makes economic sense to install super-insulation in a building that is guaranteed airtight. Otherwise the draughts will always win, and the benefit of a reduction in conduction losses through the fabric will not be realised. With both of these in place – and a healthy-buildings policy for the indoor climate – a passive-standard (zero-space-heating) requirement can often be readily achieved. This will be realised through the incorporation of extract-ventilation heat recovery, or via the use of natural ventilation where the occupants are aware of the implications of their actions in terms of internal-temperature maintenance.

There are important indoor-climate issues that follow on from creating an airtight envelope, and this does mean that attention has to be paid to toxicity in internal finishes (adhesives, paints, etc.) and to the ability of the construction to deal with humidity.

'A building that incorporates photovoltaic cells that has not been tested for airtightness, seems to be a pointless expense.'

Nick Grant

without a building being specified, designed and built (and tested) for airtightness, going to higher insulation levels – or even super-insulation – is not sensible, as the vast majority of the heat losses will be through uncontrolled draughts. placing any form of supply-side energy onto such a building is a waste of money.

Passive standard can only be achieved with guaranteed levels of high insulation and tested and approved airtightness. At the Glencoe Visitor Centre windows were sealed using sheepswool.

Building and Photo Gaia Architects

Shelter Planting:
Trees and bushes for energy conservation.

Many projects experience, during late cost-cutting, the removal of landscape elements once they get towards the end of the site operations. Suddenly, trees and bushes do not get planted because they are seen as 'amenity planting' – that is, non-essential decoration.

However, vegetation – or a lack of it – can have a very significant impact, not just on the biodiversity contribution of a development or even as a means of mopping up urban pollutants (which certain shrubs are very good at) but, importantly, on the energy performance of a building.

Trees and shrubs can shelter buildings – especially the elevational areas – from prevailing and chilling winds, with a resultant reduction in heat loss as a benefit. Bushes and trees can also exploit crosswinds, whereby in combination they can induce air to flow over or through rooms needing natural ventilation.

Of course these items have an amenity value – but with a practical (and calculable) economic benefit, they are less likely to be omitted during belt-tightening cost exercises. (These are often referred to as 'Value Engineering', which, all too often, is in fact merely a capital-cost-cutting exercise.)

the finns know about designing for wind
shelter: if they get it wrong, drifting snow will
block the front door.

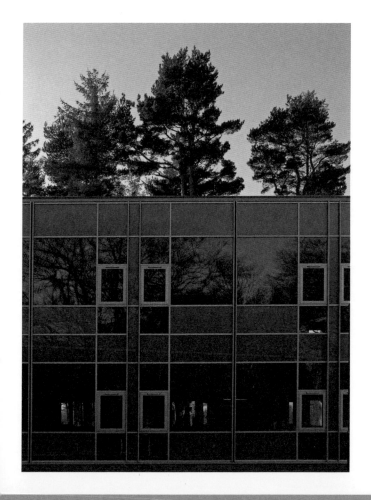

Shelter-belt planting can have a
significant impact on the energy
performance of a development,
especially if it protects from cold
winter winds, and reduces chill
effect. It can also add to outdoor
comfort around buildings.

Photo Michael Wolshover

Natural Ventilation:
Good early design can obviate the need for fans.

The employment of natural ventilation in modern buildings has been happening in experimental structures for quite a while, and client insistence on air-conditioning currently appears to be slightly on the wane. There are now a number of high-profile buildings in operation which use the stack effect or atrium design (or both) to draw air through their interiors. In central Europe and Scandinavia, there are some highly innovative projects using plants, water and natural – or naturally induced – airflows to maintain a comfortable indoor climate.

In Norway, there is even a parent-led initiative for healthy schools using natural ventilation. The thrust for this has emerged from highly positive feedback from a number of pilot schools designed by GAIA Architects in Norway, in the early 1990s.

The search for natural
ventilation solutions in larger-
scale buildings (without any
means of mechanical assistance)
has led to some very interesting
architectural solutions.

Coventry University Architect Alan
Short. Photo Sandy Halliday

fan power is more effective at moving air about
than dealing with the humidity and pollutants
it contains. a return to basic principles can be
instructive to designers.

Natural/hybrid Ventilation:
There are some innovative approaches to ventilation which minimise fan power.

here, described are two examples of innovative methods of natural hybrid ventilation which are based on the principle of natural ventilation but which sometimes require a boost.

Culvert cooling (and pre-heating)

A number of Norwegian schools have been using subterranean ventilation shafts (culverts) for their air intake, in order to obtain a benefit both in summer and in winter from taking up the constant ground temperature (around 10 °C). In winter, this reduces the demand on the heating system by introducing fresh air at a temperature often 20 °C higher than the ambient outdoor winter temperature (on average, consistently well below -15 °C).

In summer, this same process can be used to cool the outdoor air and introduce it into rooms where overheating would otherwise occur. It is sometimes necessary for the stack effect driving this system to need a little fan assistance under low-wind regimes, or in low-rise buildings where a tall enough chimney cannot be engineered simply.

Dynamic insulation

Over the past 10 years, a number of buildings in the UK – mostly sports premises or housing – have been designed to maintain their indoor 'climate' (a combination of temperature, humidity and air movement) via dynamic-insulation (also known as 'pore-ventilation') methods. Air is drawn into a room from above the ceiling through a fine membrane and the layer of ceiling insulation. As this air enters the room (through the whole ceiling area), almost as a fine, slow-moving aerosol – it has already taken up the heat that was going out through the ceiling and has also dehumidified the incoming air (warm air holds water more easily than cold air). While the natural stack effect at the extract end can be used to induce the air to go through the membrane, this system usually comprises both a (very-low-wattage) input and output fan. The pressures required to drive the system are orders of magnitude less than those required for conventional mechanical ventilation.

GAIA has pioneered a number of hybrid ventilation techniques in the UK, notably the use of dynamic insulation and culvert ventilation in leisure centres. These are based on the principles of natural ventilation but often require a little bit of low fan power assistance.

BREATHE project. Architects Rotherham City Council. Ventilation and materials consultants Gaia. Photo RCC

Earth Arches, New Guerna by Hassan Fathy. Photo Howard Liddell

Earth Arches at the Valley of the Kings, Luxor Egypt. Photo Howard Liddell

earth

element

Biodiversity:
Where does greenfield stop and brownfield start?

There are many benefits at all levels – whether local, regional or global – in seeking to increase the biodiversity of all built-environment projects.

The tendency in cities has been for green areas to be set apart rather than integrated – for example, as parks – and even then they tend to comprise swards of grass and set-piece flower arrangements in preference to habitat-creation for both flora and fauna. Oddly, much of the managed landscape that is often regarded as 'greenfield' comprises farmland that has seen very little other than monoculture for years. By contrast, brownfield sites often lie derelict long enough for nature to fight back quite well in such a context – establishing some intriguing pioneer habitats, for example, and demonstrating that such sites can actually contain more species and more diversity than ones identified as greenfield. The key challenge for designers is to ensure that they maximise the potential for a rich and diverse landscape – seeking to improve on what was on the original site in terms of the number and diversity of species, whatever the inherited context.

As maintenance-free attitudes to landscapes and our love affair with the car prevail, there is a growing recognition that there are environmental, social and economic costs to the rapid increase in the hard surfaces that always accompany such trends. Initiatives such as SUDS (sustainable drainage systems) have sought to reverse this degradation. Opportunities therefore exist both for conserving existing habitats and for creating new ones.

the city of berlin has a '50 per cent rule' for new developments, whereby half the built-up footprint of any site has to be biodiverse – it can be 'greenscape' (gardens, etc.) or 'bluescape' (ponds, etc.).

Whether it is holding on to the existing biodiversity of a site or creating new habitats, the Berlin 50 per cent rule of matching every m² of building with a m² of biodiverse landscape (also used at Malmö) is an exciting challenge.

Malmö City Council.
Photo Howard Liddell

Design for Recycling:
Anything can be recycled, but at what cost? Easy recyclability is a sustainable-design issue.

It has been mentioned in the section on 'Recycled Materials', that there is nothing that cannot be recycled – given enough time and expense. However, as well as seeking economical ways of reusing processed materials and products that were manufactured without recycling in mind, we should also be learning from previous approaches to manufacture and assembly. This would encourage us once again to start manufacturing materials – and constructing buildings and landscapes – that can be readily reused, demounted, disassembled, eventually recycled and, ultimately, benignly disposed of back to the earth.

The benefits can be more than long term – demountability also affords flexibility in the short and medium term. Knowing that plumbers and electricians are going to want to get at pipes and wires, it seems obvious that we should make it easy for them to do so without having to wreck floors, walls and ceilings. As an example, 'nail-free' construction has been developed with this in mind. Lime mortar in brickwork allows a wall to be taken down without breaking the bricks; cement mortar, being stronger than the bricks it connects, necessitates smashing those bricks at demolition, as this is easier than breaking the mortar.

Given the trend of the last 30 years towards ever-shorter lifespans for buildings, it is alarming that our methods of building have embraced ever-more permanent materials, products and construction systems.

a shinto shrine is taken down and rebuilt every 20 years as a process of spiritual cleansing. knowing this will happen affects the design

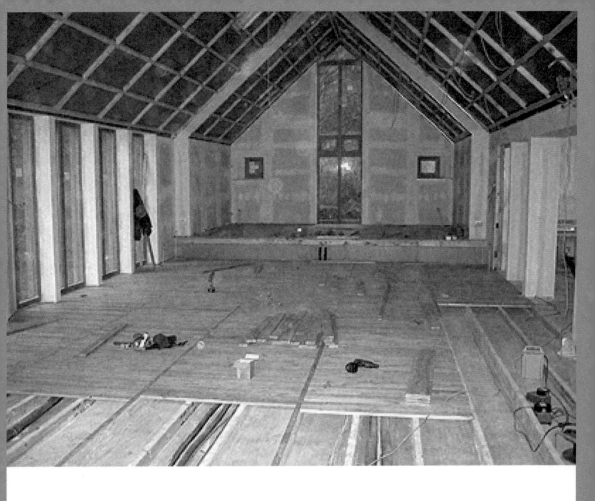

Whilst designing with recycled materials is often an expensive and sometimes self-defeating goal, learning our lesson from undemountable construction will give hope for future refurbishers. This floor at Glencoe is nail-free and the boards are held in by screw-down battens.

Gaia Architects, 2003. Photo Gaia

Benign Materials:
Only 3 per cent of the estimated 55,000 materials we currently use in buildings have been tested for their impact on human health.

Those pursuing a green design agenda often make assumptions about local materials being inherently a better choice than those from further afield. There is even a 'bio-regional' movement. The significance attributed to such materials appears to be (a) that they will contain less embodied energy in getting to the site and (b) that their purchase will contribute to the local economy.

Both of these assumptions can be undermined, however.

It is important to look at every material on its merit. If non-toxic paint is not manufactured locally, it is nevertheless important to have a benign indoor climate – and the latter should be an overriding consideration.

Once a building has been sealed up in the name of energy conservation it does not just need a policy of 'build tight, ventilate right'. There are two key areas of concern which require mitigation; the first is material toxicity and the second is humidity. A sealed building needs to have materials internally that are both benign and open porous.

given a choice between a local product with questionable health credentials and a guaranteed healthy material that will perform the same function, most parents would not spend long making a decision about which to use for decorating their nursery.

Knowing the credentials of a material is essential for ecological specification. If the designer has not been party to the procurement cycle then third-party accreditation is necessary to ensure a healthy (non-toxic) indoor climate.

Glencoe, Gaia Architects. Photo Michael Wolshover

Mass Timber:
Huge potential impact in carbon sequestration.

Modern methods of mass-timber construction developed in Switzerland over the past two decades, and expanding from central Europe to Scandinavia, have meant that low-grade timber can be brought into the building industry at rates competitive not just with other forms of timber construction but also with masonry and other heavyweight methods.

Even species such as Sitka spruce – of which there is an overabundance in the UK – can be brought into the construction industry through this technology, and perform in a way that was never before possible. For example, a 10 cm deep solid brettstapel (dowelled mass timber) plank can span up to 12 metres and can also act as a permanent, self-finished reinforcement platform for concrete.

This form of construction acts as a carbon-storage system and can be a major contributor, beyond mere carbon-neutral buildings, towards carbon-sink buildings. The chemical logic runs as follows: the CO_2 equivalent of 1 kg of wood-fixed carbon is about 3.6 kg, and, therefore, as seasoned wood is 50 per cent carbon, about 1.8 kg of CO_2 is bound into 1 kg of wood product.

This building material is pure eco-minimalism: contributing to good value for money, healthy indoor-climate credentials and a perfect strategy for carbon storage – and all invisible to the untutored eye.

One of the most promising (and most subtle) potential contributors to the carbon crunch is mass timber – which fixes 1.8 kilos of CO_2 for every kilo of timber. It takes the agenda way beyond the concept of a low-embodied-energy material to that of a carbon sponge.

Factory Sohm Holzbau material for
Acharacle school Gaia Architects.
Photo Howard Liddell

calculations in norway have indicated that a 'mode shift' from standard methods of construction to mass timber could have a more significant impact on reducing the country's carbon footprint than removing all the cars from the roads.

Maintenance:
If something is to be sustainable, it must also be maintainable.

Given that the purchase of a building is often the largest single investment an individual will make, it is quite bizarre that the concept of buildings or building products being maintenance-free has gained credence. In stark contrast, it is regarded as a positive asset for a car to have a regular service record and it is written into the purchase agreement of electronic equipment. (Of course, there is something confidence-sapping in the offer of an extended warranty from one to three years that often costs half the price of the hardware being bought!)

Why would it be smart not to have an annual external-fabric check (gutter cleaning; check on roof, windows, doors; etc.)? All that a lack of maintenance does is allow a small problem to become a big one. This usually means that the repair and replacement cost of the big problem far outweighs the equivalent cost of regular maintenance.

Many building suppliers pride themselves on having a product that is maintenance-free and does not require painting. All too often, this means that they cannot be maintained and they cannot be painted.

Change is an intrinsic part of life and of living. People's social, financial and environmental circumstances are all constantly evolving and all require constant attention if they are to thrive.

routine maintenance is an intrinsic part of good housekeeping and is an insurance against premature building-product or equipment replacement.

WINDOW CLEANING

UPVC Cleaning & Restoration

GARDEN MAINTENANCE

Grass Cutting   Hedge Trimming

This white van message rather undermines 25 years of marketing uPVC products – promoted as maintenance free. Maybe the industry has realised that it is those products that cannot be maintained that are the real problem.

Swiss hydro power. Photo Howard Liddell

water

element

Water Conservation:
Demanding less has both financial and environmental benefits.

As with energy strategies, it makes little sense, either economic or environmental, to concentrate on treatment and 'end-of-pipe' solutions before having ensured that everything possible has been done to reduce the load requiring end-treatment.

Even in high-rainfall regions, it is not the mere quantity of water being used, for example to flush WCs, that is the problem – it is the fact that this is usually potable (drinking-quality) water, which has acquired an environmental and an economic cost en route to the supplying appliances. The proportion of water being used for flushing, bathing and clothes-washing is nearly 60 per cent of an individual's daily demand in the UK.

Using dual-flush, low-flush, super-low-flush, waterless and other forms of conservation plumbing fittings, the reduction in both demand and treatment provision is dramatic and delivers both an environmental and an economic benefit.

Rainwater harvesting, grey-water recycling, composters, separating WCs and other intermediate technologies can also have an impact – but each needs to be reviewed on a project-specific basis, as it will be competing for budget with other environmental strategies.

even in areas of high rainfall, it is not merely the amount of water but the amount of (bought) drinking-quality water – most of which is used for wc flushing – that is at issue.

Whilst the UK has been dragging its feet in producing eco-products, other Europeans have simply gone ahead and created their markets. This low - flush WC uses rainwater.

W.C. Elemental Solutions. Photo Sandy Halliday

Hard Surfaces:
Rainwater – an opportunity.

Where hard surfaces are unavoidable, it is important to look at the resulting water run-off and retention. In terms of holding up the water flow, the principle of cleanliness prevails: any polluted water, such as the outflow from areas of car use, needs to be contained and not allowed to go to ground or pipes until properly trapped and filtered. In terms of rainwater retention, the use of 'swales' – whereby the impact of periods of high rainfall is mitigated by the creation of temporary ponds –
is now commonplace. Hard surfaces at roof level offer an opportunity for rainwater collection, as indeed do the elevations of high-rise buildings, which receive more rainfall than their relatively small roof areas by virtue of the fact that rain tends usually to fall at an angle to the vertical.

The use of retained water, or even water in the process of aeration, can offer amenity opportunities such as a water sculpture, waterfalls or ponds. The creative and artistic use of water is something that is much better understood and used in mainland Europe.

It is said that Birmingham has more canals than Venice (36 and 26 miles respectively) – but they are kept well hidden. The UK has developed a negative relationship with water, and has a tendency to want to fence it off rather than enjoy it.

Water is also part of the designer's climatic modification toolbox, and can help to create successful microclimates – particularly in semi-contained spaces.

if we stopped putting water down drains and played with it in the open a little more, we would not only help address the increasing incidence of flooding – we would also make better public places.

To deal with rainwater run-off, we can use the sponge or the container. Where hard surfaces are unavoidable, they can be used to good effect as a context for water engineering including scultpure.

Fairfeild. Gaia Architects.
Photo Michael Wolshover

Soft Surfaces:
Preventing flooding whilst promoting biodiversity.

Soft surfaces are a preference for the environmental-protection agencies, and increasingly important as the UK addresses climate change and increased flooding. At high level, soft roofing retains water and delays its release into the surface-water run-off system. Disparaging comments about turf roofs being an eco-cliché (see the 'Turf Roof' section in 'Technical Fix') can be reviewed if consideration of a more lightweight sedum roof can provide a genuine environmental benefit at little or no extra cost. It can also achieve delays and losses via evaporation.

Feeding gardens from path and other non-polluted run-off is another double-benefit design contribution.

Setting aside completely any discussion about congestion or pollution and focusing strictly on land-use issues, there is a discussion to be had here about the motor car's impact at ground level. Centralised and/or stacked (e.g. in a 'paternoster' parking machine), its impact can be mitigated. The author has calculated – from a selection of low-density developments – that an average two-storey house with a single garage and a single parking space has roughly equal amounts of concrete (or equivalent) hard surface for both the house and the car. This includes a footpath for the pedestrians and the backing-out space and road requirements for the vehicle. In anything other than a very low-density scheme, the extent of residual area for soft landscaping will be minimal. Moving up to a double garage and two parking spaces virtually doubles the area needed for cars; in other words, the land requirement for cars is twice that required for people. Clearly, we are 'voting with our wheels'.

it is not possible to discuss the introduction of more soft surfaces without also addressing the issue of the motor car.

Where soft surfaces are possible they should be the first choice. They usually need to make their case against the competing objective to cover the globe in asphalt.

Rainwater run-off to gardens Stroud co-ownership Housing. Architype Architects.
Photo Howard Liddell

Moisture Mass:
Absorbent finishes are nine times better than mechanical ventilation at dealing with humidity.

We are used to thinking about thermal mass – we know that the sea holds onto heat during the summer. We also know that a clay-tiled floor will hold onto solar gain better than a carpeted one.

There is an equivalent phenomenon with moisture.

Contemporary construction has moved away from buildings which have walls, ceilings and floors made from natural, moisture-open (hygroscopic) materials – such as lime plaster, timber and mineral paints – to a palette of man-made, and usually impervious, materials and finishes such as chipboard, polyurethane-coated laminate floors, emulsion-sealed plasterboard and vinyl wallpapers and floor coverings.

This trend has led to an indoor moisture problem. The humidity in the air has nowhere to go and the levels rise – creating ideal conditions for dust mites and mould, which thrive above 60 per cent RH (relative humidity – 100 per cent is a rainy day and 0 per cent is the middle of the Sahara; humans are most comfortable around 40–60 per cent).

The tendency has been to counter this with increasing quantities of mechanical ventilation – often controlled by a 'humidostat' that triggers with high levels of RH. However, mechanical ventilation is a crude tool for removing moisture. Fans are efficient at moving air around – but the vapour in the air is less compliant. Indeed, according to recent Finnish research fans are nine times less effective than hygroscopic materials (untreated timber, unbaked clay, mineral-painted lime plaster, etc.) and they also take away lots of precious warm air. By using such materials, we can 'head off the problem at the pass' – giving a whole new meaning to the term 'passive' design.

mechanical engineers can only work with what the architect gives them. if it is a glass box with impervious internal surfaces, they start on the back foot.

This building is made from hemp. Hemp is one of a number of new-old traditional materials that work extremely well as indoor humidity dampers. Clay and open-grain timber fulfil the same function

Green Light Trust Architect.
Photo Ralph Carpenter

Capital Cost

'Buildings need to get greener faster …
to regard green buildings as special may
not help the cause.'[10]

...Once dropped its is difficult to pick up again and regain lost ground

Diagram by Howard Liddell

'Read my lips'

The precepts of 'anti-bling', pro-commonsense eco-minimalism must also challenge, head on, the fallacious assumption that it costs more in capital terms to build green. At client briefings and project meetings around the country, this false premise lingers and leads inevitably to discussions about how the unsubstantiated extra 'moolah' can be justified through reduced costs-in-use or life-cycle-costing benefits. Even if I believed that such a debate was necessary – which I don't – it is rarely backed up with real evidence, and more rarely still does it result in an increased capital budget. Imagine the wasted effort and damage to relationships that accompany a fight to secure funding that, but for an eco-minimalist approach, might not actually be needed at all! It's an Alice-in-Wonderland world of shoddy thinking that has the net effect of stultifying any progress on the delivery of green buildings even before the ink is dry on project briefs. I refer to this process as 'dropping the green baton'. Once dropped, it is difficult to pick up the green baton again and regain lost ground.

On the other hand, the technical-fix approach to green buildings will cost more – because it is additive. What has been added on can all too easily be taken off, and in the vast majority of cases that is exactly what will happen if (or more likely, when) cost savings have to be achieved. It all starts with good green intentions, which then can't be afforded and so are ditched.

However, it need not be like this. In the hands of an experienced eco-minimalist designer, the good-housekeeping approach will cost little or no more because it is inclusive; it has been designed in and not on.

Let's say it again – it does not need to cost more.

'Successful solutions result from "going for it" rather than worrying about the cost-effectiveness of every single item.'[11]

We are faced, however, with a conundrum. While the myth of 'going for it' being more expensive prevails, there is a simultaneous and unresolved question as to how 'going for it' might be defined.

There is a small amount of very useful work to inform this question – and all of it confirms one key thing: that well-researched green design can actually lead to buildings that cost less. Even when it leads to more costly buildings, the extra amount is so small as to be almost irrelevant. However, this information is not getting out into the public domain.

Without proper information, we are mired in a daunting combination of ignorance and prejudice. Hence the need for this book, and its message of eco-minimalism, which aims to demonstrate that, within reason and above a minimal quality threshold, building green need not cost more. Eco-minimalism is not necessarily easy to achieve – it requires an appropriately experienced designer to be able to make the trade-offs and be selective in specification and design – but it is possible.

10 Bill Bordass, *Cost and Value: Fact and Fiction.*
11 Ibid.

The Cost of green buildings

Chart compiled by Howard Liddell

Study	Savings>	Additional Cost %>
	60% 70% 80% 90% 100%	100 101 103 104 105 106 107 108 109 110
LEED (1) Schools+Offices		< >
BREEAM Domestic / Offices		< > / < >
Austrian e.g. Ludesch centre		>
Gaia (Ind'l) Rock bottom / light green / deep green	> / >	>
Gaia Sports Centre / Housing / Vistor Centre	> / > / >	
Solarbau Datapec / WAT / Prisma	> / > / >	<Additional Cost of design
LEED (2) Academic (norm) / Academic (green) / Libraries(norm) / Libraries (green)	< > / < > / < > / < >	

Interestingly, over the 25 years of my practice producing only green buildings nobody ever gave us more money to build these for them, nor did we ask for it. We are not aware of any magic wand that has allowed us to do this in isolation from the so-called 'real world'.

Whose definition?

The following is a selection of some of the studies that have been undertaken on the relative cost of building green.

Labelled buildings

For instance, BREEAM or LEED green building 'labels'.

1 A feedback study by Cyril Sweett of BREEAM- and EcoHomes-assessed buildings demonstrated that improvements in their sustainability performance had been achieved at very little extra cost. It showed that achieving a 'good' rating in domestic projects increases the capital cost by a mere 0.5 per cent, and that for the 'excellent' rating the increase is more like 5 per cent. For offices, achieving a 'good' rating can marginally reduce the capital expenditure – and to reach an 'excellent' only requires adding 3 per cent.[12]

2 A similar study using the LEED assessment system – the US equivalent of BREEAM – showed a cost premium of 0.66 per cent ('certified') to 6.5 per cent ('platinum') for schools and offices.[13]

3 In the case of the £3 million town centre development in Ludesch, built in the Vorarlberg area of Austria in 2005, the clients commissioned a parallel study during the construction period to establish the additional cost of adopting a very high quality of Passive Design and a Healthy Building materials specification. The research report identified the additional costs for the whole project as being of the order of 3 per cent – and that for the vetted healthy-building materials (third-party reviewed by IBÖ, the Austrian Institute for Building Biology) to be a maximum of 1.9 per cent over conventional costs, with a cost-in-use benefit that paid for itself in the first few months of occupation. (This sum does not include for the cost for the third-party vetting of the materials for their health credentials.) In looking at the nature of the materials used and their availability in the UK, as at January 2008, the percentage additional costs are transferable and equivalent to UK costs.[14]

4 The £2 million Glencoe Visitor Centre in the Scottish Highlands was built in 2002 and, by careful design and selection of materials – including home-grown timber; biomass fuel heating; natural ventilation; breathing floor, walls and roof construction; demountable (nail-free) detailing; new British slate roofing; low-flush WCs

---

12 Cyril Sweett, *'Putting a Price on Sustainability'*
13 Greg Kats, *'The Costs and Financial Benefits of Green Buildings'*, a report to California's Sustainable Building Task Force.
14 Wehinger, Torghele, Mötzl, et al. *'Neubau Ökologisches Gemeindezentrum Ludesch (New-build Ecological District Centre, Ludesch)'*.

and waterless urinals – was delivered on a par with similar facilities in the UK. Its mechanical- and electrical-engineering content was reduced via a strategy of passive design, super-insulation and airtight construction to 9 per cent of the capital cost (as against a norm of around 25 per cent). The 16 per cent trade-off in unused heating, ventilation and electrical technology was used for the higher-quality fabric, including a high standard of healthy building materials. The healthy specification stipulated zero PVC, formaldehyde or VOC (volatile-organic-compound) content in materials. It included natural and untreated timber inside and out, mineral paints, cellulose fibre insulation, sheepswool caulking around windows and linoleum floor covering. Unlike the Ludesch building work, no detailed analysis or third-party vetting of materials was undertaken. The above information has been derived from the architects and quantity surveyor.

Solarbau Project

5 In Germany, where the value of additional pre-construction indoor environmental design and modelling is appreciated and valued, it has been shown to save up to 25 per cent on capital construction costs.[15] In addition it has shown up to 50% improvement in running costs when compared with equivalent conventional buildings.

The first three studies include buildings with add-ons (PVs, small turbines, etc.), and it is evident that if an eco-minimalist approach had been adopted then all three would be reporting even lower figures. The introduction to the Cyril Sweett study says: 'One of the principal barriers to [green] solutions is the perception that they incur substantial additional costs. This study contradicts this assumption.'

'Estimation procedures can often be found wanting when looking at individual green features, which can be picked off one by one as not cost effective, whereas they would hang together as a package.'
Bill Bordass

Cost/m² studies

1 A US study looked at a whole range of buildings with both green (i.e. LEED-rated) and non-green credentials, with costs ranging between £1000 and £3000 per m². Significantly, the buildings with green credentials appeared in every cost band – from 'cheap' to 'expensive'. In other words, the quality of the architecture was of far more significance, in cost terms, than whether the buildings were green or not.[16]

2 In a small study for an industrial eco-park for Scottish Enterprise, GAIA and their quantity surveyor colleagues investigated the additional cost, in low-budget industrial buildings, of constructing the units with a varying materials specification – from 'as cheap as possible', to 'light green' and, finally, 'deep green'. This study showed that at the lowest costs there was virtually nothing to trade off in order to build green. However, as the cost increased

15 The Solarbau Initiative involved three mixed-use development projects, saving between 10 and 15 per cent on capital costs and up to 50 per cent on running costs – for an extra 1 per cent in fees.
16 Davis Langdon Adamson, 'Costing Green: A Comprehensive Cost Database and Budgeting Methodology'.
17 Gaia and Ralph Ogg, 'Cost Study for Forfar Eco-park'.

McLaren Centre.
Gaia Architects. Photo Howard Liddell

to a more reasonable (and average standard) budget, the trade-offs became possible. There is, therefore, a minimum cost benchmark, below which it is very difficult to build green – but it is indeed very low.[17]

3 In feedback audits on their own buildings built between 1998 and 2003, GAIA managed to deliver projects with accredited 'high green' credentials at quite basic cost levels – i.e. with construction costs in a range between £800 and £1750 per m^2 for leisure, residential and office buildings. All of these were at no more (and sometimes less) cost than contemporary, equivalent, non-green buildings built by others.[18]

... and Benefits
Work (economy), folk (community), place (environment)

Whilst lip service is paid to the equal importance of environmental, social and economic factors, the economic are always made 'more equal' than the others. Hence the need once and for all to nail the myth about the extra capital cost of building green (see above).

Fortunately, the news gets better: once a green building has been delivered, it is win-win all over the place! Not only are costs-in-use lower than for equivalent non-green buildings, but there are plenty of other benefits too.

Win-win for work

The financial benefits of green building include lower energy, waste disposal and water costs, lower environmental and emissions costs, lower operations and maintenance costs and savings from increased productivity and health. And in terms of refurbishment:

'An initial upfront investment of up to £50,000 to incorporate green building features into a £2.5 million project would result in savings of at least £500,000 over the life of the building, assumed conservatively to be 20 years.'[19]

Win-win for folk

Studies into healthy indoor-climate design and productivity have indicated dramatic reductions in:

- Acute respiratory illness (ARI) of 23–76 per cent (worth $6bn to $14bn per year in the USA)
- Allergies and asthma of 8–25 per cent (worth $6bn to $14bn per year in reduced health costs and $1bn to $4bn in economic gains)
- Sick building syndrome (SBS) of 20–25 per cent (worth $10bn to $30bn per year)
- Direct productivity gains of 0.5–5 per cent (worth $20bn to $200bn per year)[20]

Win-win for place

The above studies indicate direct gains to individual buildings and their users. However, these gains accrue to the benefit of whole economies, whole communities and the local, regional and global environments.

18 Various GAIA in-house and commissioned third-party reports.
19 Greg Kats, op. cit.
20 William Fisk and Satish Kumar, 'Health and Productivity Gains From Better Indoor Environments'.

Tollhouse Gardens. Gaia Architects. Photo Howard Liddell

Summary and conclusions

The skilled practitioners will trade off the higher price of certain sustainable materials by moving towards passive design and away from highly serviced buildings. They will do this by employing careful orientation, massing design and detailed specification. The use of passive design, breathing-wall construction, hygroscopic finishes, natural ventilation, the elimination of air-conditioning and similar measures can all be used to reduce costs.

Such a strategy is, of course, going to be affected by the type of building in question. It should also be borne in mind that the initial cost of a building is relatively small in relation to its whole-life cost and, therefore, increased construction prices will not be particularly relevant over the life of the building unless they are of considerable magnitude. It is also necessary to consider costs holistically, as tertiary benefits (improved health, reduced absenteeism, etc.) will accrue to either the building owner or society as a whole – and ultimately both.

'Call a thing immoral or ugly, soul-destroying or a degradation of man, a peril to the peace of the world or to the well-being of future generations; as long as you have not shown it to be "uneconomic" you have not really questioned its right to exist, grow, and prosper.'
E. F. Schumacher

Postscript

This excellent book is about the technologies, broadly considered, of the buildings we live and work in, the nature and amount of energy and materials they use, and their impact on the environment. Howard's proposals are invariably practical – he was brought up on the dictum that an ounce of practice is worth a ton of theory – and some demand big changes in the value judgements and decisions of architects and builders and of policy-makers. In a world of escalating oil prices and impending shortages of supply, and where climate change is starting to make itself felt, it is imperative that the kind of research and analysis that make this book so compelling are continued.

I was fortunate enough to have Fritz Schumacher as a friend and colleague during much of my working life, and especially during two spells of work that involved the promotion of widespread changes in technology. The first was when we formed the Intermediate Technology Development Group (now renamed Practical Action) in 1964, to promote the use of small-scale, inexpensive, labour-using machines and equipment. The prevailing practice of aid-givers, now largely discredited, was to lumber poor countries with the labour-saving, high-cost technology of the rich countries. We largely succeeded in our aim, as Practical Action is now well-known internationally, is working with partner bodies in six developing countries and runs a successful consulting company and information service. We were also involved with the Soil Association, which was started in 1946 and is now a leading environmental charity campaigning for the global shift of agriculture to organic, sustainable food and farming.

Both Practical Action and the Soil Association are now influential bodies with international reputations. Both have the support of research and consultancy organisations; both publish journals and undertake educational work. At the time when they were first formed, both were either ignored or considered eccentric or plain cranky. Today they are highly regarded, except by eccentrics and cranks. I am surely not alone in believing that Howard could now create an organisation much needed by architects and builders which could quickly become as effective in its field as Practical Action and the Soil Association are in theirs. It could, to take some examples, publicise and promote best practice and pillory the worst; update knowledge of relevant research and fill gaps in knowledge by doing or commissioning research; identify issues requiring legislation, or changes in professional skills; publish material for small builders and for the public at large, or for informing clients; provide relevant material for the training of architects and builders. Its motto might be: 'An ounce of better practice is worth a ton of theory.'

George McRobie
June 2008

References/ Selected Reading

References

Carson, R *"Silent Spring"*, Houghton Mifflin Company, Boston. (1962)

Dickson, D *"Alternative Technology and the Politics of Technical Change"*. Fontana (1974)

Geddes, P *"Sciences in genera"l*. Life (1931)

Halliday, S *"Sustainable Construction"* Butterworth Heinemann (2008)

Halliday, S *"Green Guide to the Architect's Job Book"*. RIBA Publications (2000)

Liddell, H *Ecominimalism, Green Buildings Bible Vol 1* Green Building Press, pp 98-103 (2006)

Pattersoan, Walt *"The Energy Alternative: changing the way the world works,* "available on http://www.waltpatterson. org/contents.htm (1976)

Schmid, P. *"Bio-logische Baikonstruktion"* Rudolph Müller (1986)

Schumacher, E.F. *"Small is Beautiful. A study of economics as if people mattered"* Blond Briggs (1973)

Schumacher, E.F *"Good works"* Jonathan Cape (1979)

Seymour, J & S *"Self-Sufficiency"* London: Faber & Faber. (1970).

Steingraber, S. *"Living Downstream"* Virago Press, London (1997)

Vale, B & R *"The Autonomous House"* Thames and Hudson (1975)

McRobie. G. *"Small is Possible"* Jonathan Cape (1981)

4 Elements

Berge, B. *"The Ecology of Building Materials"* Architectural Press, Oxford (1999)

Halliday, S, Morrison, C. *Children's Eco City Project* Children's Parliament (2003)

Eco-Bling

BEAMA *(British Electrothechnical & Allied Manufacturers' Ass'n) Metering & monitoring of domestic embedded generation* House of Commons (28.11. 2007)

BREEAM @ http://www.breeam.org/

DTU *"Moisture Buffering of Building Materials:"* BYG°EDTU R-126 Department of Civil Engineering, Technical University of Denmark. (2005)

Jaakkola, J.J., Verkasalo, P.K. and Jaakkola, N., *"Plastic wall materials in the home and respiratory health in young children"*. American Journal of Public Health; Vol. 90 pp. 797-799 (2000)

Liddell, H. Kay, T Stevenson, F *Recycled Materials for Housing.* Scottish Homes (1993)

London Hazards Centre, *"Toxic Treatments"* London Hazards Centre (1989)

Norton, *"Heating Water by Sun"* Centre for Alternative Technology. (2000)

Oreszczyn, Tadj. *"Energy Efficiency in the UK"* at Royal Institution, Glasgow, 15 February 2006.

Eco-minimalism

Dreiseitl, H. Grau, D. and Ludwig, K. *"Waterscapes Planning, Building and Designing with Water"*. Birkhauser. (2003)

Fanger, P.O. et al *"A simple method to determine the olf load in a building"*, 5th International Conference on Indoor Quality and Climate (ndoor Air '90) Vol 1, pp 537-42 (1990)

Feynman. R P *Surely You're Joking Mr Feynman* New York, (1985).

Gaia Architects *"Light Earth Construction"*. Gaia Research (2003)

Gaiagroup *"Design and Construction of sustainable Schools Vols 1& 2"* Scottish Executive (2005)

Grant, N. Moodie, M. Weedon, C. *"Sewage Solutions"* Centre for Alternative Technology (1996)

Halliday S.P, Chapman B, Jones P and Liddell H.L. (2005) *"Affordable Low Allergy Housing"*, Gaia Research, Edinburgh ISBN 1-904-680-17-8

Houben, H& Guillard, H
"Earth Construction".
Intermediate Technology (1994)

Roalkvam, D *"Naturlig Ventilasjo"n*
NABU/NFR (in Norwegian) (1997)

SEDA Guides - *1 - Design and
Detailing for Airtightness 2 - Design and
Detailing for Deconstruction 3 – Design
and Detailing for Reducing Toxicity in
buildings* http://www.seda2.org/dfa/
index.htm

SEPA *"Designs that hold water
Sustainable Urban drainage Systems
explained."* Video (undated)
www.sepa.org.uk

One Watt standby http://www.iea.org/
textbase/papers/2005/standby_fact.
pdfPassivhaus

Cost

Bordass, B. *Cost and value: fact and
fiction,* Building Research & Information
Volume 28, Issue September 2000

Cyril Sweett, 'BREEAM - Putting a Price
on Sustainability' BRE trust (2005)

Davis Langdon Adamson, *"Costing
Green: A Comprehensive Cost Database
and Budgeting Methodology"*. (2005).

Greg K, *"The Costs and Financial
Benefits of Green Buildings"*.
A report to California's Sustainable
Building Task Force, (2003).

Lovins, A.L & von Weizacher, E
*"Factor 4 – Doubling Wealth and halving
Resources"*. Earthscan (1997)

Wehinger, Torghele, G. Mötzl, et. al.
*"Neubau ökologisches Gemeindezentrum
Ludesch"* Bundesministerium fur Verkehr,
Innovation + Technologie (2006)

William F.J., *"Health and Productivity
Gains from Better Indoor Environments
and Their Relationship with Building
Efficiency",* Annual Review of Energy and
the Environment, Vol. 25 pp. 537-566
(2000),